Life and Times of The King Cool Elvis Presley

Fun Trivia Questions, Quizzes and Personality of Famous Artist

DEDICATION

Contents

Elvis Presley

Elvis Aaron Presley[a] (January 8, 1935 – August 16, 1977), also known simply as Elvis, was an American singer, musician and actor. He is regarded as one of the most significant cultural icons of the 20th century and is often referred to as the "King of Rock and Roll" or simply "the King". His energized interpretations of songs and sexually provocative performance style, combined with a singularly potent mix of influences across color lines during a transformative era in race relations, led him to great success—and initial controversy.

Presley was born in Tupelo, Mississippi, and relocated to Memphis, Tennessee, with his family when he was 13 years old. His music career began there in 1954, recording at Sun Records with producer Sam Phillips, who wanted to bring the sound of African-American music to a wider audience. Presley, on rhythm acoustic guitar, and accompanied by lead guitarist Scotty Moore and bassist Bill Black, was a pioneer of rockabilly, an uptempo, backbeat-driven fusion of country music and rhythm and blues. In 1955, drummer D. J. Fontana joined to complete the lineup of Presley's classic quartet and RCA Victor acquired his contract in a deal arranged by Colonel Tom Parker, who would manage him for more than two decades. Presley's first RCA single, "Heartbreak Hotel", was released in January 1956 and became a number-one hit in the United States. With a series of successful network television appearances and chart-topping records, he became the leading figure of the newly popular sound of rock and roll.

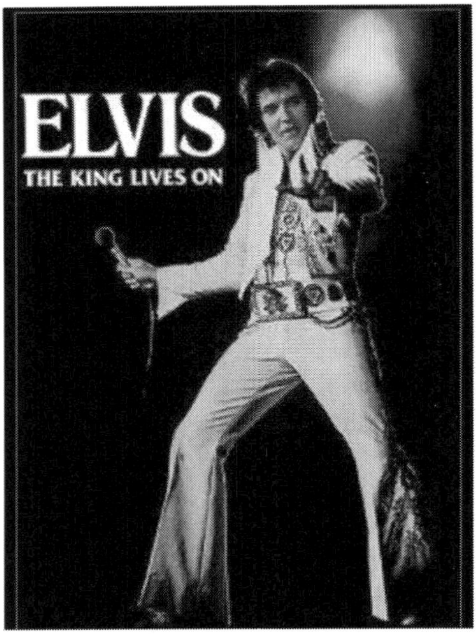

In November 1956, Presley made his film debut in Love Me Tender. Drafted into military service in 1958, Presley relaunched his recording career two years later with some of his most commercially successful work. He held few concerts, however, and guided by Parker, proceeded to devote much of the 1960s to making Hollywood films and soundtrack albums, most of them critically derided. In 1968, following a seven-year break from live performances, he returned to the stage in the acclaimed television comeback special Elvis, which led to an extended Las Vegas concert residency and a string of highly profitable tours. In 1973, Presley gave the first concert by a solo artist to be broadcast around the world, Aloha from Hawaii. Years of prescription drug abuse severely compromised his health, and he died suddenly in 1977 at his Graceland estate at the age of 42.

With his rise from poverty to significant fame, Presley's success seemed to epitomize the American Dream. He is the best-selling solo music artist of all time, and was commercially successful in many genres, including pop, country, R&B, adult contemporary, and gospel. He won three Grammy Awards, received the Grammy Lifetime Achievement Award at age 36, and has been inducted into multiple music halls of fame. Presley holds several records; the most RIAA certified gold and platinum albums, the most albums charted on the Billboard 200, and the most number-one albums by a solo artist on the UK Albums Chart and the most number-one singles by any act on the UK Singles Chart. In 2018, Presley was posthumously awarded the Presidential Medal of Freedom.

Trivia Quiz - Ultimate Elvis : Part 1

1. Elvis had a twin brother who died at birth. What was his name?

Vester Garon

Jesse Garon

Vernon Garon

Johnny Garon

2. Which song did Elvis close the "1968 Comeback Special"? (He wore a white suit)

American Trilogy

Can't Help Falling in Love

If I Can Dream

Guitar Man

3. Who directed the 1970 documentary film "Elvis - That's The Way It Is"?

Steve Binder

Herbert Soklow

Denis Sanders

Colonel Tom Parker

4. In which film did Elvis play the part of Ted Jackson?

Easy Come, Easy Go

Double Trouble

It Happend at the World's Fair

The Trouble With Girls

5. What was the name of Elvis' private Jet?

Answer:

(Two Words)

6. What was Elvis' Army serial number from 1958 to 1960?

53310761

10330761

83310861

09330861

7. Who owned "Sun Records" where Elvis started his recording career?

Colonel Tom Parker

Steve Sholes

Elvis Presley

Sam Phillips

8. In which Elvis song can you hear the following lyrics: "Make me feel at home, if you really care, scratch my back and run your pretty fingers through my hair" ?

Stuck on You

Treat me Nice

Fame and Fortune

Anyway You Want Me

9. In which movie did Elvis sing "I Slipped, I Stumbled, I Fell"?

Change of Habit

Wild in the Country

Loving You

G I Blues

10. Elvis had a pet chimpanzee, what was his name?

Scooter

Scatter

Lucky

Charlie

11. In the film "Blue Hawaii" Elvis was cast as who?

Steve Grayson

Chad Gates

Rusty Wells

Mike Windgren

12. In which Elvis song can you hear the following lyrics?: "A million years it seems, have gone by since we shared our dreams. But I'll hold you again, there'll be no blue memories then." ?

Blue Moon

All That I Am

My Happiness

She Thinks I Still Care

13. How much did Elvis purchase his home "Graceland" for?

$200,000

$75000

$100,000

$150,000

14. Elvis' first film was "Love me Tender". NOT including the two documentary films, do you know what his last feature film was?

The Trouble With Girls

Change of Habit

Charro

Live a Little, Love a Little

15. How many films did Shelley Fabares appear in with Elvis?

1

4

2

3

16. In which film did Elvis sing the song "One Track Heart"?

Girl Happy

Roustabout

Clambake

Girls! Girls! Girls!

17. Who took over the role as Elvis' manager after Scotty Moore?

Sam Phillips

Bob Neal

Colonel Tom Parker

Joe Esposito

18. Elvis was in the middle of filming which movie, when he got a

letter from "Uncle Sam"?

King Creole

Love Me Tender

Jailhouse Rock

Loving You

19. In which Elvis song can you hear the following lyrics: "Well, if you ever go, darling I'll be oh so lonely. I'll be sad and blue, crying over you, dear only." ?

Loving You

That's When Your Heartache Begins

Little Darling

Love Me

20. How old was Elvis when he died?

41

42

51

52

21. By the end of the year 1977, how many "Number One" British singles did Elvis achieve?

18

12

17

15

22. "The Elvis Medley" consisted of excerpts from "Jailhouse Rock", "Teddy Bear", "Hound Dog", "Don't Be Cruel", "Suspicious Minds", and which other song?

Can't Help Falling in Love

Moody Blue

Burning Love

Heartbreak Hotel

23. How many movies of the "Elvis movies" were made in black and white?

2

None

1

3

24. "Hawaii" was the setting for how many of Elvis' films?

3

2

4

1

25. In which Elvis song can the following lyrics be heard: "Just when I think I know her well, her emotions reveal, she's not the person that I thought I knew." ?

Way Down

I'm not the Marrying Kind

Moody Blue

Stuck on You

ANSWERS

1. Elvis had a twin brother who died at birth. What was his name?

Answer: Jesse Garon

Jesse Garon was delivered dead, thirty five minutes before Elvis was born.

2. Which song did Elvis close the "1968 Comeback Special"?
(He wore a white suit)
The correct answer was If I Can Dream

The single "If I Can Dream" was released shortly before the televised TV Special.

3. Who directed the 1970 documentary film "Elvis - That's The Way It Is"?
Answer: Denis Sanders

A new version of "Elvis-Thats The Way It Is" was released in the year 2001 which included over 30 minutes of unseen footage which was not used in the original film, and was named "Elvis - That's The Way It Is Special Edition".

4. In which film did Elvis play the part of Ted Jackson?
The correct answer was Easy Come, Easy Go

"Easy Come Easy Go" was Elvis' twenty-third film, and was released in 1967.

5. What was the name of Elvis' private Jet?
The correct answer was Lisa Marie

The Convair 880 Jet was bought by Elvis in 1975.

6. What was Elvis' Army serial number from 1958 to 1960?
Answer: 53310761

Elvis' mother passed away while Elvis was serving in the Army.

7. Who owned "Sun Records" where Elvis started his recording career?
The correct answer was Sam Phillips

RCA Purchased Elvis' contract from Sam Phillips in 1955.

8. In which Elvis song can you hear the following lyrics: "Make me feel at home, if you really care, scratch my back and run your pretty fingers through my hair" ?

Answer: Fame and Fortune

The correct answer was Treat me Nice

Elvis sang "Treat me Nice" in this third movie "Jailhouse Rock".

9. In which movie did Elvis sing "I Slipped, I Stumbled, I Fell"?
Answer: Wild in the Country

"Wild in the Country" was Elvis' seventh film released in 1961.

10. Elvis had a pet chimpanzee, what was his name?

Answer: Scatter

Scatter eventually became violent, and was caged behind Graceland, and that's where he eventually died.

11. In the film "Blue Hawaii" Elvis was cast as who?
Answer: Chad Gates

Elvis was cast as: "Steve Grayson" - Blue Hawaii, "Rusty Wells" - Girl Happy, "Mike Windgren" - Fun in Acapulco.

12. In which Elvis song can you hear the following lyrics?: "A million years it seems, have gone by since we shared our dreams. But I'll hold

you again, there'll be no blue memories then." ?
Answer: My Happiness

The first song that Elvis recorded at the Memphis Recording Service was "My Happiness".

13. How much did Elvis purchase his home "Graceland" for?
The correct answer was $100,000

Elvis purchased Graceland in 1957.

14. Elvis' first film was "Love me Tender". NOT including the two documentary films, do you know what his last feature film was?
Answer: Change of Habit

Elvis played Dr. John Carpenter in the film "Change of Habit". The two final films were the documentaries:- "Elvis - That's The Way It Is" and "Elvis on Tour".

15. How many films did Shelley Fabares appear in with Elvis?
The correct answer was 3

Shelley Fabares appeared in "Girl Happy", "Spinout" and "Clambake".

16. In which film did Elvis sing the song "One Track Heart"?

The correct answer was Roustabout

"Roustabout" was released in 1964 and also starred Barbara Stanwyck.

17. Who took over the role as Elvis' manager after Scotty Moore?

The correct answer was Bob Neal

Elvis, Scotty and Bill were known as the Blue Moon Boys back in the 1950's.

Legendary guitarist Scotty Moore was Elvis' first manager.

Bob Neal was Elvis' manager from January 1955 to March 1956.

18. Elvis was in the middle of filming which movie, when he got a letter from "Uncle Sam"?

The correct answer was King Creole

The Memphis Draft Board granted Elvis a sixty day deferment in order to finish the movie "King Creole"

19. In which Elvis song can you hear the following lyrics: "Well, if you ever go, darling I'll be oh so lonely. I'll be sad and blue, crying over you, dear only." ?

The correct answer was Love Me

Elvis sang "Love Me" on "The Ed Sullivan Show" and in his 1973 concert "Elvis: Aloha From Hawaii".

20. How old was Elvis when he died?
The correct answer was 42

Elvis died on August 16th, 1977 at his Graceland home.

21. By the end of the year 1977, how many "Number One" British singles did Elvis achieve?
The correct answer was 17
Elvis' last "Number One" single by the end of 1977 was "Way Down".
In the year 2002 the single "A Little Less Conversation" reached the number one spot, his 18th Number One single (The Beatles have had 17 "Number One" singles).

22. "The Elvis Medley" consisted of excerpts from "Jailhouse Rock", "Teddy Bear", "Hound Dog", "Don't Be Cruel", "Suspicious Minds", and which other song?
The correct answer was Burning Love

Elvis can be heard singing excerpts from some of these songs in the

"1968 TV Special"

23. How many movies of the "Elvis movies" were made in black and white?
The correct answer was 3
"Love me Tender", "Jailhouse Rock", and "King Creole" were all filmed in black and white. Many years later a colour version of the film
"Jailhouse Rock" was released on VHS.

24. "Hawaii" was the setting for how many of Elvis' films?
The correct answer was 3
"Blue Hawaii", "Girls! Girls! Girls! and "Paradise Hawaiian Style".

25. In which Elvis song can the following lyrics be heard: "Just when I think I know her well, her emotions reveal, she's not the person that I thought I knew." ?
The correct answer was Moody Blue

Elvis recorded "Moody Blue" in 1976 at Graceland.

Trivia Quiz - Ultimate Elvis : Part 2

1. In what year did Elvis receive the U.S. Jaycees Award?

1972

1971

1970

1969

2. Elvis married Priscilla Beaulieu in a private ceremony at Palm Springs, California?

True

False

3. In which film did Elvis play the part of Steve Grayson?

Speedway

Kid Galahad

Clambake

Easy Come, Easy Go

4. In which movie did Elvis sing "A House That Has Everything"?

A Change Of Habit

Clambake

Girl Happy

Follow That Dream

5. In which Elvis song can you hear the following lyrics: "We had the chance to fall, but fate stepped in to end it all, before it could begin"?

Have I Told You Lately That I Love You

Almost

All That I Am

Almost In Love

6. Who allegedly said the following: "Every time I felt low, I just put on an Elvis record and I'd feel great, beautiful."?

Frank Sinatra

John Lennon

Paul McCartney

Elton John

7. "Me 'N Elvis" was an autobiography written by Charlie Hodge?

True

False

8. In which Elvis song can you hear the following lyrics: "Hold my hand and promise that you'll always love me true. Make me know you love me, the same way I love you little girl."?

I Beg Of You

Home Is Where The Heart Is

Hey Little Girl

Stuck On You

9. Gladys Presley can be seen in which of Elvis' movies?

Loving You

King Creole

Love Me Tender

Blue Hawaii

10. How many Elvis films were produced by Hal B. Wallis?

Eight

Two

Nine

Twelve

11. How many people, is it said, watched "Elvis: Aloha From Hawaii" in 1973?

One Million

Fifty Thousand

Ten Thousand

One Billion

12. What was Elvis' birth weight?

6 Pounds

7 Pounds

4 Pounds

5 Pounds

13. In which Elvis song can the following lyrics be heard: "Come to these arms, these arms that need you. Don't close your eyes to my plea."?

Lover Doll

Loving Arms

Don't Leave Me Now

Loving You

14. In which film did Elvis play the part of Jess Wade?

The Trouble With Girls

Flaming Star

Charro

Stay Away Joe

15. "Guitar City", "So I'll Go Quietly" and "Pot Luck" were just three of several titles considered for which of Elvis' films?

Kid Galahad

Speedway

Clambake

Frankie and Johnny

16. From January 1967 onward, what was Colonel Parker's share of Elvis' income?

50%

75%

25%

60%

17. What was the name of the jet that Elvis gave to Colonel Tom Parker as a Christmas present in 1975?

Falcon Jet

Presley Jet

Lisa Marie 2

Eagle Jet

18. Who did Elvis allegedly say was his favourite actress of those with whom he had worked?

Juliet Prowse

Ann Margaret

Shelley Fabares

Joan Blackman

19. In which Elvis song can you hear the following lyrics: "God shed his grace on thee, and crown thy good with brotherhood, from sea to shining sea"?

America the Beautiful

How Great Thou Art

Saved

Shake a Hand

20. Graceland is located in which Memphis suburb?

Answer: Whitehaven

(Not Black)

Trivia Quiz - Ultimate Elvis: Part 3

1. Most of us know Elvis was born in a shack in Tupelo, but can you name the road/street?

Poplar Avenue

Audobon Drive

Alabama Street

Old Saltillo Road

2. Elvis attended Humes High School from 1948 to 1953.

True

False

3. In the 1970 documentary "Elvis - That's The Way It Is", who sent Elvis a note reading: "Here's hoping that you have a very sucessful opening and break both legs"?

The Beatles

Colonel Tom Parker

Tom Jones

Frank Sinatra

4. Elvis' TV Special "Elvis: Aloha From Hawaii" was a benefit concert for the Kui Lee Cancer Fund.

True

False

5. The Last Will and Testament of Elvis A Presley was signed and sealed on which date?

8th January 1977

3rd March 1977

16th August 1976

3rd November 1975

6. Elvis purchased a Convair 880 Jet in 1975 which he named "Lisa Marie"

What was the purchase price?

$750,000

$250,000

$1.5 million

$50,000

7. When were the bodies of Elvis and his mother Gladys moved from Forest Hill Cemetery to the Meditation Gardens at Graceland?

16th August 1978

10th October 1977

2nd October 1977

8th January 1978

8. Four of the five pallbearers at Elvis' funeral were Joe Esposito, Lamar Fike, Charlie Hodge and Billy Smith. Who was the fifth?

Vernon Presley

Dr. George Nichopoulos

Felton Jarvis

George Klein

9. Pepsi Cola was Elvis' favourite soft drink.

True

False

10. How many tiers were there on Elvis and Priscilla's wedding cake?

5

7

4

6

11. In which film did Elvis play the part of Danny Fisher?

Loving You

King Creole

A Change Of Habit

Flaming Star

12. In which Elvis film did Joan Blackman play the part of Maile Duval?

Kid Galahad

It Happened at the World's Fair

Roustabout

Blue Hawaii

13. What was Elvis' thirteenth film?

It Happened at the World's Fair

Roustabout

Kissin' Cousins

Fun in Acapulco

14. In which film did Elvis sing the song "One Track Heart"?

Roustabout

Clambake

Speedway

Girl Happy

15. What part did Elvis play in the 1967 film "Double Trouble"?

Steve Grayson

Guy Lambert

Rusty Wells

Mike McCoy

16. In which Elvis song can you hear the following lyrics:
"Just put in two bars of stardust, just hang out one silly moon"?

Five Sleepy Heads

Fools Rush In

Fools Fall in Love

Fairytale

17. In which Elvis song can you hear the following lyrics:

"You know the papers told of how you lost your life, oh yea"?

Beginner's Luck

It's Easy for You

Long Black Limousine

I Feel So Bad

18. Elvis sang "I Was the One" to Shelley Fabares in the movie "Girl Happy".

True

False

19. There were quite a few cancelled concerts just before Elvis's death and obviously just after. Where was Elvis due to appear on the 17th and 18th August 1977?

Utica, New York

Baton Rouge, Louisiana

Portland, Maine

Memphis, Tennessee

20. What is Elvis wearing on the album cover of "A Touch Of Gold"?

Red Shirt

Black Leather Suit

Gold Lame Suit

White Jump Suit

Elvis Presley Trivia Questions & Answers

1 In 1957, after performing in Vancouver and Toronto, Elvis was scheduled to perform in Montreal. But the concert was canceled. Why?
Answer: The Catholic Church forced the cancellation of the concert.

Believing Elvis to be a bad influence, the Catholic Church in Montreal forced the cancellation. It was one of many instances where the Church took a strong stand against Elvis, including the suspension of eight girls at a Catholic school in Ottawa because they violated an oath not to attend his concert there.

2 What was the day, month, and year of Elvis' first commercial record release?
Answer: 19 July 1954

"That's All Right (Little Mama)", Elvis' first recording session, was booked on July 6, 1954. Most remember the famous now legendary story of Elvis, Scotty Moore, and Bill Black, taking a break from recording, and Elvis ad-libbing to Arthur "Big Boy" Crudup's song. Producer/owner of Sun Records, Sam Phillips, ran into the recording area, and asked what the boys were doing. "We don't know" was their basic reply. "Well, whatever it is do it again". Those other dates: 10 May 1956: Elvis' first recording session for RCA. 30 June 1953: Elvis would graduate from Humes High School around this time. And 8 January 1956 is a day EVERY Elvis fan recalls: Elvis' birthday.

3 From where did Elvis get his Christian name?
Answer: It was his father's middle name

The name "Elvis" was his father's middle name. Elvis' father, Vernon Elvis Presley, was born in 1916 and his mother, Gladys Love Smith in 1912 and they married in 1933. Elvis's identical twin, Jesse, was stillborn.

4 Elvis had a twin brother who was stillborn. What was his name?
Answer: Jesse

After Jesse Garon was stillborn, Elvis was born within minutes. The two were born on January 8, 1935.

Question created by team player JoeTrivia55.

5 In 1956 Elvis sang about "Suede Shoes", but what colour were they?

Answer: Blue

Elvis recorded "Blue Suede Shoes" in 1956. Carl Perkins wrote the song and recorded it prior to Elvis.

6 What age was Elvis when he died?

Answer: 42

Elvis passed away in the early hours of the morning at his Graceland home on the 16th August 1977. Some people claim he had been taking prescription drugs because he was slowly dying of bone cancer. However, this has not been confirmed.

7 Complete this well known quote from Elvis Presley: "Man, I was tame compared to what they do now. Are you kidding? I didn't do anything but just _________ ."

Answer: jiggle

From the press conference in New York City 1972, which was prior to Elvis' Madison Square Garden shows.

11 Most of us know Elvis was born in a shack in Tupelo, but can you name the road/street?

Answer: Old Saltillo Road

Old Saltillo Road was later given the address of 306 Old Saltillo Road and is presently 306 Elvis Presley Drive.

12 At what time was Elvis Presley born?

Answer: 4:35 a.m.

He was born at 4:35 A.M., 30 minutes after his brother. His brother, Jesse Garon, was stillborn. Throughout Elvis's life, he believed he could talk to Jesse.

13 In what year did Elvis receive the U.S. Jaycees Award?

Answer: 1971

"10 Outstanding Young Men of America Award" was given to Elvis by the U.S. Jaycees on January 16, 1971.

14 In what year did "Elvis: Aloha from Hawaii via Satellite" take place?
Answer: 1973

The concert took place on January 14, 1973, in Honolulu, Hawaii, at the Honolulu International Convention Center. Proceeds from the show went to the Kui Lee Cancer Fund.

15 Elvis was born in Tupelo, Mississippi on January 8, 1935. Elvis had a twin brother who died at birth. What was his name?
Answer: Jesse Garon

Vernon and Gladys Presley gave birth to twin boys on January 8, 1935. Jesse Garon died at birth. Elvis' parents were highly protective of their remaining son and raised him with strict religious tenets in the Assembly of God church.

16 "A Boy Like Me, A Girl Like You" featured in which film?

Answer: Girls! Girls! Girls!

The film Girls! Girls! Girls! was produced by Hal Willis and directed by Norman Taurog and is from 1962.

The title song was by Lieber and Stoller the same guys who wrote "Jailhouse Rock". It features the Jordanaires burping in the background!

17 It's 1954, Elvis, Scotty Moore and Bill Black begin performing their first professional shows for, can you believe $10.00 a night? What was the stage name given to Scotty Moore and Bill Black?
Answer: Blue Moon Boys

The trio encountered tremendous success in country and western clubs across the south and southwest. Many owners of the clubs they played considered the boys too wild. Reception from radio stations wasn't too favorable either. Blues stations thought the act was too country for their listeners. Country stations felt the boys were too bluesy.

18 What is the name of Elvis's first #1 hit song?

Answer: Heartbreak Hotel

His first #1 hit song was "Heartbreak Hotel," released on January 27, 1956, and recorded on Januray 10, 1956.

19 Elvis had a twin brother who died at birth. What was his name?

Answer: Jesse Garon

Jesse Garon was delivered dead, thirty five minutes before Elvis was born.

21 What item was Elvis said to collect from every city he performed in?

Answer: Police Badge

On occasion Elvis would dress in a police uniform and patrol the Memphis freeways, presumably wearing one of his badges, and stop motorists when he considered they were driving irresponsibly.

22 In what year was Elvis born?

Answer: 1935

Elvis was born on January 8, 1935 in Tupelo, Mississippi.

23 What year did Elvis marry?
Answer: 1967

Elvis married in the now infamous Paisley suit.

24 This 'hareless' classic canine caper was written by Jerry Lieber and Mike Stoller in 1952. It was first performed by Elvis on Uncle Miltie's television show in 1956 and became an instant hit. Then as the 'tail' goes, Elvis repeated his performance on Steve Allen's show with the real article! But no, her name wasn't Shirley! What song did he perform?
Answer: Hound Dog

March 28, 2002 has brought us another sad loss, American television personality Milton Berle also passed away at 93. Elvis was considered a little wild for TV but the kids obviously loved this song! You could even say they 'lapped' it up! The first recording of this song was by 'Big Mama' Willie Mae Thornton in 1953. The subsequent Steve

Allen show appearance was with a Bassett hound. Bad joke huh? Shirley Bassett? Rumor has it that Ed Sullivan really didn't want Elvis on his show and then when he saw the reactions, he had to break down and invite him, though only to be seen above the waist so as to avoid offending delicate sensibilities!

25 What role did Dutch born Andreas Cornelis van Kuijk play in Elvis' career?
Answer: Manager

Cornelius van Kuijk is better known as 'Colonel' Tom Parker. He changed his name after he fled to the U.S.

26 What is Elvis' full name?
Answer: Elvis Aron Presley

He had a twin brother, Jesse Garon, who was stillborn, leaving Elvis to grow up as an only child.

.

27 What was the name of Elvis' private jet?

Answer: The Lisa Marie

Elvis' private jet was named after his daughter, Lisa Marie.

28 Who was Elvis' right hand man?
Answer: Joe Esposito

Joe Esposito was Elvis' right hand man. He was with Elvis to the day he died.

29 Who is Elvis' double first cousin?
Answer: Patsy Presley

Patsy Presley is Elvis' double first cousin. Her mother was Gladys' sister and her father was Vernon's brother. Thanks to JDavis3874 for providing me with Patsy's married name.

30 How old was Elvis when his mother died?
Answer: 23

Gladys Love Presley died in 1958. Shortly before her son was shipped to Germany.

31 One of the first backing musicians in Elvis's early recording days was ____________ ?

Answer: Winfield Scott Moore

Better Known as 'Scotty Moore' on guitar.

32 When was Elvis born?

Answer: January 8, 1935

Elvis was born on January 8, 1935 in Tupelo, Mississippi.

33 When Elvis met his future wife, Priscilla Beaulieu, how old was she?

Answer: 14

Elvis met Priscilla, the daughter of an Air Force Officer, when he was in the US Army and stationed in Freidberg, Germany., in 1959. After seeing her in a nightclub, he arranged for a friend of his to ask if she would like to meet him, and to bring her to his home. Elvis took a liking to her immediately.

When he returned to the US after being discharged from the Army in March of 1960, they had an on and off long distance relationship until 1962. When Elvis suggested she finish her schooling in Memphis, her father reluctantly let her move.

They married in Las Vegas in May 1967, and had one daughter, Lisa-Marie. Some suggest that Elvis lost interest in Priscilla once she was a mother, which is the reason for her affair with a karate instructor. They divorced in 1973.

34 When was the day, month, and year of Elvis' official final commercial release (in his lifetime)?

Answer: 19 July 1977

The title of his final studio album was "Moody Blue." Elvis Presley recorded all the studio track recordings at his home, Graceland, in the den area, which the fans would later refer to as "The Jungle Room." The title track of this album, "Moody Blue", topped the Country Music charts, on February 19, 1977. The Saturday, August 13, 1977 edition of "Billboard Magazine" posted the LP "Moody Blue" at number 24 on the Top 200 charts. Release dates and other interesting information about our man's recording career and music chart successes can be found in several books dedicated to this subject, one of which is Ernest Jorgensen's "Elvis: A Life In Music."And those other dates: 8 January 1977 was Elvis' 42nd birthday. 26 June 1977 was Colonel Parker's birthday, and the date of Elvis' final concert performance, and one of the saddest days in music history: 16 August 1977, the day Elvis said "Goodbye." Rest In Peace Elvis.

35 What were the titles of both sides of the first record Elvis cut - the one for his mother's birthday?
Answer: "My Happiness" and "That's When Your Heartache Begins"

He had to make another record for the other side of his first proper record in order for it go out on the Southern record charts.

36 What year was an Elvis recording first played on radio?
Answer: 1954

The first Elvis recording ever played on radio, in 1954, was "That's All Right". The B side was "Blue Moon of Kentucky." It was played on radio WHBQ by DJ Dewey Phillips, located in Memphis, USA. This recording brought widespread attention to Elvis, and the rest, of course, is history.

37 Elvis was born in which town?
Answer: Tupelo, Mississippi

Elvis attended Milam Junior High, until his family moved to Memphis, Tennessee in 1948. They wanted to search for a better life.

Question created by team player JoeTrivia55.

38 In Elvis' 1968 TV "Comeback Special", what was the colour of the leather suit he wore for most of the show?
Answer: Black

In the TV Special Elvis wore a two piece black leather suit while jamming on stage with his band. There is also a segment of the show where he stands alone in the centre of the state singing a variety of his hits, in the same black leather suit.

39 Excluding the two documentary films, how many movies did Elvis star in?
Answer: 31

Elvis' first film was "Love me Tender" in 1956.
The two documentary films:
"Elvis, That's the Way it is" and "Elvis on Tour" were the two last films.
"Elvis on Tour" being his 33rd film.

40 "The image is one thing and the ____________is another, it's very hard to live up to an image." What is the missing word from the

above sentence quoted by Elvis?

Answer: human being

This was also said at the press conference at Madison Square Garden.

41 Where was the first house that Elvis bought located?

Answer: Audobon Drive

Elvis bought this house for his mother. His parents did not even have to cut the grass because the crazed fans would take pieces of it as souvenirs.

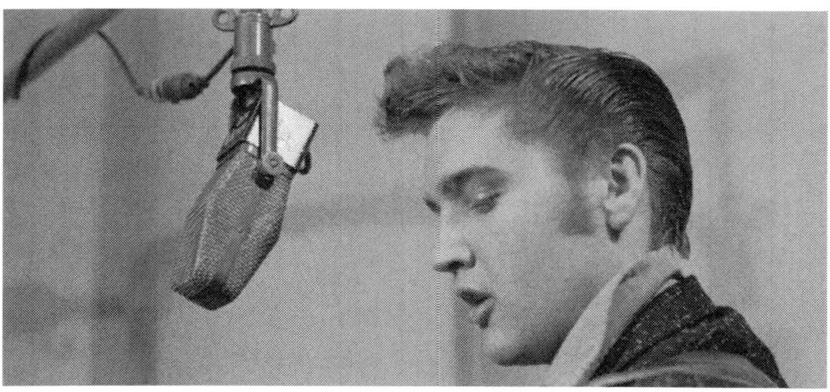

42 How did the Presley family spell Elvis' name on his tombstone?

Answer: Elvis Aaron Presley

The correct spelling on both Elvis' birth certificate and tombstone is

Elvis Aaron Presley; however, Elvis did spell his middle name "Aron." His father had them spell Elvis' middle name Aaron on his tombstone because Elvis preferred the traditional spelling of Aaron.

43 What was the first tune played at the Aloha concert?
Answer: Also Sprach Zarathustra

"Also Sprach Zarathustra" was played at most of Elvis's concerts in the 1970s. It is the theme of the movie "2001: A Space Odyssey". "See See Rider" was the first song he performed, but that's not what the question said, now was it?

44 In July of 1953, Elvis decides to record his mother a record as a surprise birthday present. One song was "That's When Your Heartaches Begins". What was the flip side to this record?
Answer: My Happiness

This recording was not heard by the infamous Sam Phillips when it was originally recorded. The office manager of Sun Records, Marion Keisker, left a note for Sam Phillips stating that Elvis had a great feel for ballads. Phillips had wanted a white artist who had the black sound, and these songs, covers of The Ink Spots classics, certainly had the feel he was going for. By the way, Elvis' birthday recordings cost him $4.00 to record.

45 What was the flip side of "That's When Your Heartache Begins"?
Answer: All Shook Up

"All Shook Up" was recorded in January 1957 at Radio Recorders in Hollywood. It featured Scotty Moore, Bill Black, D J Fontana, The Jordanaires and Dudley Brooke on piano.

46 What is the name of Elvis's mother?
Answer: Gladys
Elvis's mother's name was Gladys, who died on August 14, 1958.

47 Which song did Elvis close the "1968 Comeback Special"? (He wore a white suit)
Answer: If I Can Dream

The single "If I Can Dream" was released shortly before the televised TV Special.

Printed in Great Britain
by Amazon

72706613R00035